Nature Study Hacking
Stars & Skies

Created by Joy Cherrick

Copyright © 2019 Joy Cherrick
All rights reserved.
ISBN-10: 1797641506
ISBN-13: 978-1797641508

All designed and formatted by Joy Cherrick

This publication is a creative work protected in full by all applicable copyright laws, as well as by misappropriation, trade secret, unfair competition and other applicable laws. No part of this book may be reproduced or transmitted in any manner without permission from Joy Cherrick, except in the case of brief quotations embodied in critical articles or reviews. All rights reserved.

NatureStudyHacking.com

Thanks to Kevin for taking the kids to the aquarium and
picking up the groceries so I could write.

Thanks also, Cindy, Jeannette, Joyce and Rochelle for inspiring me, supporting me and humoring me.
This series is a result of friendship.

Finally, thanks to my mom for editing, watching kids and telling me to "go for it."

Introduction to Nature Study	3
Nature Journal Prompts	19
Moon's Phases Phenology Wheel| Lesson 1	24
Moon's Phases Vocabulary| Lesson 2	26
Moon's Phases Demonstration| Lesson 3	27
Moon Poem| Lesson 4	29
Moon Poem Continued| Lesson 5	30
Moon - Reading| Lesson 6	31
Review, Improve & Delight| Lesson 7	32
Moon Phenology Wheel| Lesson 8	34
Big Dipper and Little Dipper - Story| Lesson 9	35
Big Dipper and Little Dipper - Drawing| Lesson 10	36
Review, Improve & Delight| Lesson 11	38
Cassiopeia's Chair - Story | Lesson 12	39
Cassiopeia's Chair - Drawing| Lesson 13	40
Perpetual Journal Entry| Lesson 14	42
Orion - Story| Lesson 15	43
Orion - Drawing| Lesson 16	44
Stars Poem| Lesson 17	46
Planets - Drawing| Lesson 18	47
Review, Improve & Delight| Lesson 19	49
Sun Makes a Shadow| Lesson 20	50
Sun Makes a Shadow Continued| Lesson 21	51
Sun Makes the Seasons| Lesson 22	52
Perpetual Journal Entry| Lesson 23	54
Review, Improve & Delight| Lesson 24	55
STARS & SKIES| Exam Week	56
Poems about Stars & Skies	57

Introduction to Nature Study

"The child must not be left to discover everything for himself;
his mind must be prepared in some measure for what he is to see and observe.
It has been well said that the previous history of the mind
determines the impression which the sight of any object is to make.
"We can only see what we have been trained to see."
The Parents' Review, *"How to Best Study Nature"* by Mr. J. C. Medd, M.A.

When I started my homeschooling journey sometime around 2009 or 2010, my mom sent me copies of *For the Family's Sake* and *For the Children's Sake* by Susan Schaeffer Macaulay. It was through these books that I discovered and adopted the philosophy of Charlotte Mason. Mason's ideas about educating a whole person were like a soothing balm to my soul. How did I miss that true learning involves the things that I find engaging in the world? Why had I fallen into the trap of chasing academics alone? I am so grateful and forever indebted to the unmarried school teacher, Charlotte Mason. Her life's work was to be a student of the ways of children, watch how they learn, seek out the very best for them and then, share what she learned.

The study of nature is one of the habits that sets apart the Charlotte Mason method from other literature-based or classical educational philosophies. I have done my best to get my children out-of-doors (as Mason puts it) with great regularity. We have lived most of our parenthood in subdivided neighborhoods with two glorious years spent in a farmhouse and then in a house in the woods. I know that it is much easier to get outside and explore nature when there is a generous feast just beyond the kitchen window calling to me. We are once again living in a subdivision, and I've had to develop some tools to help me continue getting our children introduced to nature so that they too will be able to call the trees, flowers and birds by name so that they will know they are friends.

As a small child, my family spent two years living on one acre squished between a herd of cattle beyond one fence and a circus horse and pony on the other. It was in this home that I was able to see my first bird's nest and chrysalis, and I became intimately acquainted with the daffodil, which remains my favorite flower to this day. I'm sure I watched some Sesame Street while living there, but my most vivid memories are of my time spent exploring our country acre.

During times of stress, loneliness and upheaval, I've always found restoration and solace in nature - be it animals, birds, trees or flowers. They seem to remind me of God's unchanging stability. They help me remember how small I am and how vast God is. Such comfort and joy. I credit much of this love and intimacy with nature to my mother's love of it herself and getting to spend unscheduled time out in it as a young child.

As Anna Comstock poetically describes in Handbook of Nature Study:

> "Nature-study cultivates in the child a love of the beautiful; it brings to him early a perception of color, form, and music. He sees whatever there is in his environment, whether it be the thunder-head piled up in the western sky, or the golden flash of the oriole in the elm; whether it be the purple of the shadows on the snow, or the azure glint on the wing of the little butterfly. Also, what there is of sound, he hears; he reads the music score of the bird orchestra, separating each part and knowing which bird sings it. And the pattern of the rain, the gurgle of the brook, the sighing of the wind in the pine, he notes and loves and becomes enriched thereby."

And we all sigh collectively and agree, that YES, this is what we want to learn to sense, experience and even express if it is in our ability to do so. Even if we have just a small bit of this level of love and intimacy with nature, we and our children will be certainly closer to what God created us as humans to be and experience from life.

So, what is nature study exactly? Why is it worth interrupting my school day in order to be sure it gets done? How should I get started? What is involved? Do I really have to read about the subjects we are studying each term? Why should I plan out our nature studies? Can't I just learn about things as we go?

Let's explore these questions and see if we can find a few helpful answers. I'm certainly not a nature study expert. But, I am passionate about introducing children and their grown-ups to nature. I also enjoy finding ways to make things simple so that I will actually do them. "A goal without a plan is just a wish," penned French writer Antoine de Saint-Exupery. So, if nature study is your goal, I will reveal a modest plan to help you and your children not only begin studying nature together, but also start a nature journal and hopefully, make the study of nature a habit that you and your children will make your own and enjoy freely. That is what has happened in our home, and it is my prayer that it will happen in yours!

> *The world is so full of a number of things, I'm sure we should all be as happy as kings.*
> - Robert Louis Stevenson

Nature Study Defined

Through him all things were made;
without him nothing was made that has been made.
John 1:3

What Nature Study is and what it is not is important to determine before we go on.

> **na·ture**
> /ˈnāCHər/
> Noun
> the phenomena of the physical world collectively, including plants, animals, the landscape, and other features and products of the earth, as opposed to humans or human creations.

So "nature study" is the study of the physical world collectively or the study of all things visible created by God. We use our senses when we study nature. We don't break apart, analyze or deconstruct, we observe the whole so that we may know it. Here's a helpful definition:

> "Nature Study, as a process, **is seeing the things that one looks at, and the drawing of proper conclusions from what one sees.** Its purpose is to educate the child in terms of his environment, to the end *that his life may be fuller and richer*. Nature Study is not the study of a science, as of botany, entomology, geology, and the like. That is, it takes the things at hand and endeavors to understand them, without reference primarily to the systematic order or relationships of objects. It is informal, as are the objects which one sees. It is entirely divorced from mere definitions, or from formal explanations in books. It is therefore supremely natural. **It trains the eye and the mind to see and to comprehend the common things of life; and the result is not directly the acquiring of science but the establishing of a living sympathy with everything that is.**" (Emphasis mine.)
> From "*Leaflet I: What Is Nature-Study?*" written by Liberty Hyde Bailey.

And so I am treading carefully when I attempt to provide a guide for mothers to better lead children into the joys of Nature Study. The spontaneity and "supremely natural" aspects of nature study are helpful to keep in mind as we try to get a handle on the practical habits we need to form to:

1. Take our children out regularly for the purpose of Nature Study

2. Decide what do we do while we are out there

3. Figure out how to actually use those charming Nature Journals without ending up frustrated and annoyed at our little darlings.

All of this, can be accomplished with less resistance if the children are following the lead of a mother who is herself seeking to learn. In fact, Nature Study is one of the areas in family life where the children and the parents can be co-learners. There has been many a time when my children notice, recognize or name something we've discovered where I am in complete ignorance. It is truly satisfying once this happens because you know that they are starting to take the responsibility of self-education. In this co-learning role, a mother can lead with her enthusiasm and wonder. Such as simply asking "I wonder where that squirrel lives?" or "I wonder why those caterpillars are all crossing the road together?" These questions may be difficult to find on Google, but I am always surprised at how much not knowing encourages deeper learning. As Anna Comstock (*Handbook of Nature Study*) put it "the object of the nature-study teacher should be to cultivate in the children powers of accurate observation and to build up within them understanding."

Now that we've explored what Nature Study is, it is important to look more closely at "WHY" we should include it in a STEM/STEAM world. You might ask, "can't they just google it and find out what something is?" or perhaps you think there is not a utilitarian purpose for Nature Study as in "what can they DO to earn money with this information?"

In a world where truth is always being muddled and manipulated, it is important for our children to encounter truth as a matter of habit. For the child, Comstock tells us, "Nature Study cultivates in him a perception and a regard for what is true, and the power to express it. All things seem possible in nature; yet this seeming is always guarded by the eager quest of what is true. Perhaps half the falsehood in the world is due to lack of power to detect the truth and to express it. Nature study aids both in discernment and in expression of things as they are."

When our family is able to learn about The Way Things Are together and does so as a regular rhythm of our family life, then we are getting the opportunity to experience and talk about the little things that truly matter with our children. There is so much in nature that can teach us lessons about getting along with others, death, procreation, colors, war, peace, beauty, weather, truth etc. All of these are available lessons if we are willing take the time to pay attention.

Another way that the study of nature is valuable is that it has been the inspiration for arts, music and dance. All throughout recorded history, we find the relationship with mankind and nature reveals our need of it and closeness to it. Of course our food source comes from nature. And our lives are forever entwined with it even though we seem more separated from the inconveniences of nature. We also miss out on becoming intimately familiar with its ebbs and flows unless we take the time to be outside regularly.

The reality is, we could live all our lives never encountering nature at all. You could stay inside your home all day and when you leave from your garage, head to a store or church and walk inside never touching the soles of your shoes to dirt. On the days that I don't get outside for one reason or another, I know that I missed something. I certainly missed the sunrise or sunset, but I also missed the birds playing or the squirrels jumping through the trees. I may have missed the flowers bloom and fade. All this is nothing I think about or even think I miss. But for some reason if I take time to pursue those little moments, my day is better. It makes me feel smaller or more poetic. Sometimes I feel that I'm getting to witness God at work in the midst of a mundane day.

Perhaps the most important reason to develop the habit of studying nature is to cultivate wonder and learn more about God. We can learn about God's attention to detail when making the tiny ant. Or what about His creativity when making insects that engage in metamorphosis and change from one type of creature to another? We can also learn about God's love for His creation as we learn about how He has equipped us for work. "Look at the birds of the air," we read, "they neither sow nor reap nor gather into barns, and yet your heavenly Father feeds them." (Matthew 6:26) Surely we are of more value than these. We can also simply sit in awe of God by watching a sunset or listening to the waves breaking on the shore. He is great and we are small. We are weak and He is strong. All of these old lofty ideas become intimate truths we claim and agree with as we learn more about the world He created for us to live in, work in and learn about Him through.

"But ask the animals, and they will teach you,
or the birds in the sky, and they will tell you;
or speak to the earth, and it will teach you,
or let the fish in the sea inform you.
Which of all these does not know that the hand of the LORD has done this?
In his hand is the life of every creature and the breath of all mankind."
Job 12:7-10

Roles

I will be a lion
And you shall be a bear,
And each of us will have a den
Beneath a nursery chair;
And you must growl and growl and growl,
And I will roar and roar,
And then--why, then--you'll growl again,
And I will roar some more!
Wild Beasts, by Evaleen Stein, 1863-1923
from *Child Songs of Cheer*, 1918

Mother's Role in Nature Study

Mother as a Guide

When I first began trying to figure out just exactly HOW to do Nature Study with my children, I heard mothers say to do it casually: "just do it when you are outside with your children" or "it will just happen as you go." Well, friends, that NEVER happened. I was always wrangling or distracted by one thing or another. In addition, it's too overwhelming to go out into The Wide World without a plan.

You need a plan.

Your plan will begin with one topic to look for when you go out. Trees? Birds? Wildflowers? Clouds? Weather? **Pick ONE!** You may want to get all fancy and add a subcategory. Don't do that, not at first. You need to actually get STARTED studying nature, and choosing ONE topic to study will help you get focused and have a sense of purpose to your time spent in nature. This is especially true if you are new to a region or new to learning to call things by name.

Once you choose your topic, say "trees," you will notice how many trees in your neighborhood that you can't name. That is ok! In fact, that means you are on the right track. Humility is essential to learning. From here, you will want to read a little bit about the topic you selected. (If you can't find time, then find a book you will read to your children ABOUT your topic so that you can all begin learning about it together.) The absolute best place for a mother to start is to read the section in _Handbook of Nature Study_ on the topic you've selected. This may take two or three sittings (remember you are only reading about ONE TOPIC (don't get overwhelmed thinking that you have to read the whole tome!)), but it is full of worthy information that will help you talk with your children about how trees live and grow and how trees differ from one another etc.

If you only have time to read to your child to learn about trees, I recommend _The Tree Book for Kids and Their Grownups._ This book will explain how a tree eats, what photosynthesis is, and it also has some delightful stories about some of the more common North American Trees. As you read to your children, it is really best if you only read one or two pages from this book at a time. This is because they introduce new concepts and explain some of the scientific terms. Sometimes that's cool and sometimes nobody but mother cares. This too is just fine. Your education matters too! You can take some of this new knowledge on the road with you.

With your book learning under your belt, it is now time to go outside WITH your children. Charlotte Mason emphasizes this in Home Education, and I know that sometimes it is easy to ignore this as "charming" or "idealistic." But, going out into nature with your children is not JUST good for them. _It is good for you too, and it is good for your relationship with them_. I enjoy taking a daily walk with my children. We don't go far, just around our block. But this little habit has brought so much restoration and healing to us and has saved many days.

Let's review:
1. Pick the ONE topic you are going to study this term or year.
2. Read up a little about this topic so that you get acquainted with basic terms and categories. You can focus on how it eats and reproduces.
3. Go outside WITH your children.

Now that you are outside with your children, let's talk about your attitude. Are you dressed properly for the weather? If you are going into the woods, are you wearing the proper shoes so that you aren't squeamish about meeting various wild creatures? We all have varying levels of comfort here, so let's assume you are walking on a sidewalk in your suburban hood. Please be dressed comfortably for the weather and elements you will face. (If you need more outerwear, I've had good luck just asking friends if they have unused things like raincoats or umbrellas. Even rain boots and snow gear can be easily found at thrift shops or online consignment for great prices. This is an investment in your family. If you have the right gear, you will find a way for your children to get the right gear as well).

Attire is the first step, but you will also need to remember that you are a co-learner with your children. Your wonder and curiosity will rub off on them, if it's genuine. I think that a simple desire to learn is all that is required.

Please do not be a stick-in-the-mud or have a grumpy attitude for the entire outing. Set your expectations ahead of time. Let them know how to meet them. And, if they are very young or very new to exploring, then it may be helpful to spend the first five minutes practicing your guidelines. (For instance, they may not cross the street without you. Or no running ahead where they can't be seen. Or, you may need to let them know that they are not allowed to play in the creek during this trip because you are in the middle of the school day and they will be free to come back after lessons. etc.) This is basic classroom management, but when it's our own children, it's very easy to forget that we need to tell them what we expect of them and then we end up putting out fires instead of enjoying the outing.

Now that you are properly dressed and you are wearing a smile on your tired face you are ready to head outside and see what comes your way. Though field days are lovely and necessary, I think that a regular outing around the place where you live can teach you and your family so much about the seasons in your area and plants that grow there. You may even end up making dear friends.

We did just this when we lived on top of a mountain. We met a woman who has become a good friend, and she kept the most glorious garden. She had many native species and had resolved to have blooms in her garden for Spring, Summer and Fall. Because of our daily walks, we were able to learn the names of many plants and birds and see many that I had only learned the name of and never met in person. We even got to see some monarch caterpillars "in the wild" eating milkweed leaves. What a gift for us all!

Mother as co-learner

Now that you are outside *with* your children and you have a topic, it is time to talk about guiding and studying alongside your children. You certainly won't have all of the answers and this is good. One way to model humility is to actually be brought low enough to realize how much we truly don't know. Which is so very much. One phrase that will work on your own mind and the minds of your children is…

"I *wonder*…"

When you wonder about things out loud, it can become a bit of a game.

This is not time to get out your phone and start googling.

I know it is tempting, but for now, just wonder. Let the questions you encounter out in the *wild* work on you all during your time outside together. When you get home or have a natural break, and the question is still working on your minds, then you can see if there is an answer. Sometimes there are only theories. That is fun too.

You may wonder: "I wonder what makes some mushrooms red and some white?" or "I wonder what a wasp eats?" Or, "that flower is beautiful, I wonder what it's called?" (You can take a photo and look it up later.)

One time, we had been reading about bugs and had just learned about a spit bug. On our walk, we saw a stalk of grass at about eye level with a wad of spit resting between the stalk and the leaf blade. I was excited and said, "I wonder if there is a bug hiding inside that glob of spit!" I broke off a piece of grass and inserted it into the spittle. Sure enough, a little black bug was hiding inside. We returned him to his place, but we were now empowered with new information. We now can pass by a spit glob on a branch or grass and know that the little occupant is hiding away inside.

As a student, you will be making your own connections. You may even get excited enough to learn a few things on your own. This is great! Don't feel like you have to deliver a lecture to your scholars about all that you've learned. Some of your new knowledge will be gradually shared over time. Sometimes, you may assault your husband or friends with your new information. Great! It's fun to learn new things. Just don't get too frustrated if your scholars don't seem to care as much as you. In our home, enthusiasm catches, but it seems to have a lag-time. Perhaps it's three months? Perhaps it will be years and years. But you loving and learning about nature will if nothing else, teach them what it is to learn about and love a thing.

The Child's Role in Nature Study

Child as Observer

It's important to understand what your goals are for your scholars as you study nature together. In general, ***your main objective is that they will be able to notice the world around them*** with the hope that they will be able to call trees and flowers by name and have a general understanding of the way God's creation works in harmony (or cacophony) with one another.

Your goal is NOT to *make them* love nature study. It is NOT to force them to memorize lists of trees or flowers or seeds. It is not to drill the kingdoms or phylum or species of each thing they encounter. You will be leading them to nature. The leading is what you can control. They will take what they will take. What affections they develop are not up to you. Don't be discouraged if they aren't excited about what you are excited about. That's normal.

As you go out into nature and study it, remember that your chief objective for your scholars is that they would become aware of their surroundings and be able to observe nature for themselves. You may play a game if that is helpful.

Charlotte Mason, in her book *Home Education*, explains a memory game to help encourage observation and also develop oral composition skills. Lead the children into nature. Then, ask them to look around at all they see. Tell them to be careful to make a note of everything. Then, close their eyes and describe it all back to you. Take turns and see who can catch the most details and explain through all your five senses. What do you see? What do you hear? What do you smell? What do you feel? What could you taste?

Your child's role here is to simply be aware and observe. It is a delight to find that children can often remember much more than we can. They can even help us discover new things right under our noses.

Child as Co-learner

The most satisfying consequence of my decision to become more intentional with Nature Study has been seeing my children taking the reigns of their own learning. Whether it's pouring over encyclopedias or mimicking my Nature Journal entries, I can tell that they see me. But they have their own interests as well.

Sometimes a child's interest will be peaked during an outing or a reading. We can encourage or dampen this tiny spark. As you would for a friend, you will be able to learn and grow and even give your child tools to learn more.

We've found that having books about the topic we are studying prominently displayed is important. Sometimes I'll face out these books on the shelf which makes these books more likely to be picked up. Then, my readers are able to read for themselves about their areas of interest. Often, they will read to non-readers and help them also gain more knowledge apart from mother. This self-education in a non-academic area is so important that it will also spread into other subjects.

Often, we will be learning about something and need to head to the map to see where in the world it comes from. From that discovery, we may find out about a war or a historic event that happened in that region, and this may lead us to learning yet another thing. Often, our studies are not easily tucked away into neat little boxes, but they bleed over into many subjects.

A Child Set Free (with purpose)

Going outside with your children for 10-20 minutes each day can't be too much. Mothers need the sunshine and fresh air just as well as children. We also need to give our children time where they are free from our watchful eye to explore, climb, dig, etc.

In America, it is increasingly difficult to find children playing outside in neighborhoods together. Most of them are tucked safely inside their homes, glued to one blue light or another. If you are reading this, you are likely one of the few parents who crave less screen time and more time outside for your children. The first step to getting them comfortable playing outside for long stretches is for you to be outside with them. Often, what happens when you go out with your children is they see that the outside isn't so bad. In fact, it is much more exciting than the walls inside. If they are having trouble staying outside, be sure they are properly dressed and go outside with them at first. Then you can slowly wean them off of needing you. Hand them a tool such as a shovel or a rope. Both of these can provide hours of interesting play for most children.

If you use screens regularly in your home, you may need to require a certain amount of time outside prior to allowing access to a screen. I have a hard rule that on beautiful days everyone must be outside. If I need to be in the kitchen or attend to the baby, I'm usually longing to join them because great weather refreshes me to the bone.

When children are outside without you, they are able to experiment and play in a way that is different from when you are on your walk with them. They may discover a bird's nest or an ant climbing up their favorite tree. Sometimes my children will stop to watch the birds near our home and thus learn about their manners and habits. These unstructured moments are so valuable to the developing child because it allows them to not only learn about the world God created first hand, but they are developing their executive function -- they are making decisions for themselves about what they will or will not do. This is a skill that is almost non-existent in most students graduating from college. They've spent their entire childhood being told what to do and where to go so that when the real world requires that they make some decisions, many adults flounder. It's very frustrating for employers looking to hire good people.

Anyway, let them play and get dirty and don't hang over them assaulting them with stories about broken bones or broken necks. If you are that worried, set some limits, say your prayers and trust them to stay within the boundaries you've laid out. All will be well. And even when it isn't, all will be well.

In His hand are the depths of the earth, and the mountain peaks belong to Him.
The sea is His, for He made it, and His hands formed the dry land. Psalm 95:4-5

Journals

*O Lord, how manifold are your works!
In wisdom have you made them all;
the earth is full of your creatures.
Here is the sea, great and wide,
which teems with creatures innumerable,
living things both small and great.
Psalm 104:24-25*

One of the biggest hangups for getting my kids to use their nature journals on a regular basis was that the majority of recommendations were to bring journals out into the field and draw something while on the outing. For me, always with a very small baby and a troublesome toddler in tow, I found it torturous and frustrating to try to guide my scholars to select their specimen to draw in their nature journals. Then, to actually draw the specimen (and not a car or princess) and then color it the color God made it and not a rainbow of colors that simply never happened consistently. Why would I subject myself to this madness?

So, for a while, I stopped trying to get nature journals to happen at all.

As a listener of [The Mason Jar Podcast](), I heard Cindy Rollins say several times that she would simply have her children draw from nature journals while she was reading aloud. This, I could do! Sitting at a table and drawing from nature books would allow me to easily see everyone and would allow us to be a little bit more organized, plus they could hear me. Finally, they could have their colored pencils ready and not risk dropping them all over kingdom come.

This simple idea of doing nature journals inside the home sitting around the table planted a seed for me. I then started exploring how modern naturalists use their nature journals. My favorite resource is [Keeping a Nature Journal]() by Claire Walker Leslie and Charles E. Roth. The ideas you see here combine the work and experience from this book with the work of Anna Comstock in [Handbook of Nature Study]() and, of course, the ideas found in Charlotte Mason's writings about this topic. To get me started I decided to use [Ambleside Online's Nature Study rotation]() selections for the current year to eliminate decision fatigue.

Now, the purpose of using the nature journal at home is to TRAIN your children how to use a field journal on their own at a later date. Laurie Bestvater encourages us in her book *The Living Page* that "the Nature Journal will have to be presented by the teacher at first… as the student gradually becomes the self-learner who relies on this companionship unconsciously." For some children this training may be a few years. For others, your structured time with nature and journaling may ignite their interest and they may start picking up their journal on their own. One of my children, within the first 12 weeks of having a plan, began picking out poetry to write into the nature journal about the current month, and later I caught that same child sketching a few different trees into the nature journal. Another child was taken by our study of the stars and planets and decided to draw an unassigned constellation into the nature journal. This shows me that we are on the right track, though my instruction will continue.

My goal is to give my children the tools they need to keep a nature journal as adults. I'm not even concerned if they decide to keep a nature journal in their adulthood or not. But, I know there will be times when they will be alone, times when they will need to focus their thoughts and ideas or even escape. If keeping a nature journal will help them, I want it to be an option. And this is why it's important that we have a plan to train the habit of using the nature journal regularly and also to teach what elements are available to be placed into a nature journal. (Hint: every subject can be utilized to study nature.)

A nature journal can be used out in the field AND can also be used inside the walls of your home. I prefer to get our kids started using a nature journal in the home at a table both *after* we've gone out and explored or perhaps even *in preparation* for an outing **to train our eyes for what to look for and help us to pay closer attention to what we see**.

"It would be well if we all persons in authority, parents and all who act for parents, could make up our minds that there is no sort of knowledge to be got in these early years so valuable to children as that which they get for themselves of the world they live in. Let them once get touch with Nature, and a habit is formed which will be a source of delight through life. We were all meant to be naturalists, each in his degree, and it is inexcusable to live in a world so full of the marvels of plant and animal life and to care for none of these things."
Home Education by Charlotte Mason pg. 61

Out-of-Doors

Never be within doors when you can rightly be without.
Charlotte Mason, *Home Education*

There are several ways in which I strive to get our children out into nature regularly. And, I confess, that even though I love to get out, even though it enriches my life, it is still a discipline to do it with regularity. What I mean is that I often don't want to go out of the house and can find a thousand excuses. The baby's schedule, my toddler has a cough, the dishes, the laundry etc all call to me as more important. And of course there is the weather. It keeps changing and once I get into a rhythm with one season, it changes and I have to adjust our patterns. I often have to coach myself to just leave the mess and get out because it is good for us all. And we all benefit by happier countenances.

The most helpful way for me to get started is to find something to go "check on" each day or each week. At one home we lived in, everyday we checked on a puddle that was in the back of a cornfield behind the property where we were living. The temperature was around 20 degrees (F) at this time, but the puddle would freeze and melt with the changing weather patterns. What we found was that the ground would also freeze into a hard rock and get slushy and muddy as the winter's rhythm progressed. Though this was not something I planned, it is a lesson that we refer back to often and even run across this type of weather and ground in the stories that we are reading. My older children have a point of reference from this experience. And these lessons that nature teaches are carried with us. All we needed to do was show up and pay attention.

At another home we lived in there were several different options, and my pattern was to take a different route each day. We checked on our neighbor's flourishing garden one day and then there was Woods Wednesday where we would check on the woods behind our home. Then on the other days, there was a route the kids could ride their bikes and yet another route where we could "check on the lake" that connected to the end of our street. There are just four days because there was usually a day for an outing with friends or our Bible Study day. I enjoyed the variety, but that is not always available.

In our current home, we only have one or two routes and they are a bit underwhelming. But still, we've seen amazing displays from the seasonal changes. One maple tree changed to a brilliant fuchsia. The biggest challenge has been our toddler. I've needed to carry, coax and discipline this child to come along with us at times. This does cut into the enjoyment of the outing, but usually when this happens I get to witness the love of siblings and find some creative ways to parent us back to the house. Usually the goal of petting the neighbor's cat does the trick. It's certainly not always "a walk in the park!"

When we have a specific topic we are studying, I will naturally draw attention to it and test myself to see if I can remember the names. Usually, I have to ask my children whose memories prove to be more faithful than mine.

It may be important to point out that ***there isn't a formula that works for everyone*** all the time to be able to do nature study consistently. Nature Study, instead, is a habit to cultivate -- especially for those of us for whom this way of living and paying attention to nature is new. As Charlotte Mason talks of education as an atmosphere, discipline and life we can see how these three principles play out in the context of nature study. The atmosphere is dictated by mother's attitude (and of course the attitude of the children as well, but mother leads). The discipline is the structure of a routine to get out into nature and the plan of what to study (which includes planning ahead by having the proper resources and books available to study). The life is the joy and the play, the messing in the dirt or the inspiration found in the stream or flower or even the new discovery made. This is exciting and life-giving for everyone.

I recently noticed that my mother and I have similar affections for flowers and nature. There seems to be a link and a passing along a love for nature that has happened without any real design on the part of my mother. And she shared with me that her mother and grandmother also loved pointing out beauty in nature and passed on a love of making flower arrangements. My great grandmother grew up in Germany, and in her village there was an abundance of flowers to enjoy. My mother told me this the other day:

"My mother was always pointing out beauty in nature. She always had some flowers planted. I remember in Virginia, we had a screened-in back porch and mother planted morning glories of all colors to climb up strings from the bottom to the top of the screen outside. In the summer mornings, I remember how beautiful they were and also with the dew on the spider webs in the yard. We were fortunate that we had a whole area of creek and woods behind our house that mother freely allowed us to roam—which we did!! We played Tarzan sometimes. I remember seeing the beauty of a passion flower out in the field and thinking it was the most beautiful flower I had ever seen. My sister also has the same love of flowers and making arrangements."

Isn't it wonderful that something so simple and so life-giving can bear fruit long after your life ends? May we persevere little by little, day by day. This idea is not new. Charlotte Mason affirms this same idea: *"Every human being has the power of communicating notions to other human beings; and, after he is dead, this power survives him in the work he has done and the words he has said. How illimitable is life! That the divine Spirit has like intimate power of corresponding with the human spirit, needs not to be urged, once we recognise ourselves as spiritual beings at all."* (School Education, pg. 71)

A note on group outings:
Group outings are so refreshing and helpful for mothers and children alike. With six children of various ages and stages, I've found that I can commit to one large group outing per month. I have several knowledgeable friends who have taught me how to identify different types of trees and different flowers. This helps *me* in the long run be a better guide at home or on family nature hikes.

During the month of April, our group scheduled something each week because it was peak wildflower season. This was just right. I love having a whole month dedicated to getting outside regularly with friends. What a gift!

The Tables Turned
By William Wordsworth

Up! up! my Friend, and quit your books;
Or surely you'll grow double:
Up! up! my Friend, and clear your looks;
Why all this toil and trouble?

The sun above the mountain's head,
A freshening lustre mellow
Through all the long green fields has spread,
His first sweet evening yellow.

Books! 'tis a dull and endless strife:
Come, hear the woodland linnet,
How sweet his music! on my life,
There's more of wisdom in it.

And hark! how blithe the throstle sings!
He, too, is no mean preacher:
Come forth into the light of things,
Let Nature be your teacher.

She has a world of ready wealth,
Our minds and hearts to bless—
Spontaneous wisdom breathed by health,
Truth breathed by cheerfulness.

One impulse from a vernal wood
May teach you more of man,
Of moral evil and of good,
Than all the sages can.

Sweet is the lore which Nature brings;
Our meddling intellect
Mis-shapes the beauteous forms of things:—
We murder to dissect.

Enough of Science and of Art;
Close up those barren leaves;
Come forth, and bring with you a heart
That watches and receives.

Nature Journal Prompts

Once you've picked out your topic, you will want to start using your nature journal to record your findings, start drawing or even finding poetry to describe the parts of nature you grow to love more deeply. I've included a list here of types of entries that you may include in your journals. You will notice that they aren't all of the drawing variety. As I've studied naturalists, I've found that some love to write words in their journals, some love to draw and date their art and some make lists or track measurements and statistics. In fact, there are as many ways to enter information into a nature journal as there are subjects to study. But, that's a bit overwhelming when we are starting out, isn't it? So here, I am giving you some ideas for types of entries to make in your journals. You can see it as a menu. Take what you like and leave what you don't. I've included the list on one page so that you can print it out separately to use for reference if you so desire.

At the end of this booklet, I've also included weekly lesson plans for those who would like a guide to get you started without the burden of deciding what to do next.

1. Copywork: Anatomy Page (Science/Language Arts/Art)
    a. copy parts and draw a diagram from a model
    b. parts of a flower/tree/horse/eye

2. Copywork: Theme Page (Science/Language Arts/Art)
    a. copy classification types/sizes/shapes etc (i.e. leaf shape, various angles of subject, bird feet types, tree shapes, caterpillar/chrysalis/larvae/eggs/plant it eats etc)

3. Draw Specimen: Label with common name, label with Latin name (Art, Language Arts)
    a. find an interesting fact about a subject
    b. Draw parts - i.e bud, flower, leaf, bark pattern, whole shape

4. Narration: (mother record's into Nature Journal if child is too young to write well) (Language Arts)
   From a recent nature outing, record the date and location then:
    a. What did you see and where?
    b. What were the weather conditions?
    c. What did you like?
    d. What did you not like?

5. Narration: Observe a habitat - draw or write about what else lives in/on/around/under/with your subject (Science/Language Arts)

6. Rubbings, tracings and pressings (Art)

7. Phenology wheel month-by-month/day-by-day (Science)
    a. Select something with a cycle to observe
    b. Caterpillars, trees, phases of the moon, weather patterns etc

8. Phenology wheel to track one subject throughout the year (Science)

9. Find a poem about the subject and copy it into your Nature Journal (Language Arts)

10. Track growth or patterns with a bar graph (Math)

11. Learn the history of the tree you are observing, use an encyclopedia, reference book or search the Internet with you parents. Record your findings on your page.

12. Draw a map
    a. Your home, favorite hiking spot, layout of a garden, neighborhood walking route and notable plants/animals/birds you encounter

How to Use This Book

Nature Study Hacking is designed to help you guide your student through the art of studying nature and keeping a Nature Journal. These principles are old, but this application is new. The ideas from Anna Comstock's classic book *Handbook of Nature Study* are combined with the ideas of modern naturalists and educators such as Clare Walker Leslie, Charles E. Roth, Cindy Rollins and Jeannette Tulis.

The lessons are designed to be short. They begin with observation. In observing nature first-hand, we begin to develop a relationship with it that can't be duplicated. This is because we are able to engage the totality of our five senses and get to know a thing in its home. I know that when I have friends over to my home they are able to know and understand me more fully. This is the same with nature.

Diagrams are used to show or label to help teach us to call nature by name. When we know the name of something we, once again, develop a closer relationship with it. We *know* it. The lessons use copywork in order to help us remember and to know. This should be a delight and a means to the greater end of learning about nature.

With care, I've woven in a variety of types of Nature Journal entries into this book. Copywork, vocabulary, writing, math, map-making, research, reading and more are incorporated so that as you study your chosen topic, you can also explore it on a variety of levels. In addition, keeping a Nature Journal is not just about painting beautiful watercolor paintings. You will enjoy learning about many different types of entries as you go through our study together! I've designed the lessons with the aim of two lessons each week over a twelve week term. However, you can do as many or as few as you'd like. My goal is to help you establish the habit of using a Nature Journal. This book is the support to help you achieve this. It's designed to serve families first and foremost.

Lastly, throughout the study you will enjoy a few "breathing lessons." I've titled them "Review, Improve & Delight." These help us and our students to take the time and care to go back over our work and add to it, clean it up and make it better. The habit of taking the time to carefully improve our work can help us not only review what we have done, but also help us enjoy what we've done and find ways to improve it.

We'd love to hear about how you are nature study hacking! Please use #naturestudyhacking on social media if you are enjoying your booklet! Please contact us at www.naturestudyhacking.com with questions, hive fives and any ideas for improving this valuable resource for families beginning their own Nature Study Hacking journey!

Setting up Your Nature Journal

Nature Study Hacking means that there are tricks and tips to share with you to make your life simpler!

Before you begin studying and journaling you will first need to set up your journal. Be sure to use a pencil and have your eraser handy when you first start laying out your pages so that you can erase markings easily. This is YOUR notebook, you are going to be working little by little to add to it just how you'd like. If you'd rather draw or paint something on a separate sheet of paper, cut it out and paste it into your notebook, you are welcome to do that. If you'd like to write directly into your notebook, that works as well! Just remember we are all learning a NEW way to use our Nature Journals, so mistakes are part of the learning process!

Supply List:
1. Minimalism Art Dot grid notebook (8.5/11 size preferred for younger children)
2. Ticonderoga pencils
3. Prisma colored pencils (preferred for younger children)
4. Preprinted Phenology wheel sliced into 32 pie pieces for each day month (plus one space for the month's name)
5. Scissors
6. Tape or glue
7. Protractor (optional if making phenology wheel instead of printing/copying it from book)
8. The night sky, sun and moon
9. Book about the Moon, Stars, Planets and Seasons (See Resources page for recommended readings)
10. Night Sky App (point at the sky and it tells you what star/planet/constellation you are observing!)

Step 1: Now that you have your supplies, open your Nature Journal. The first page on the right of most books is called the "Title Page". This is where you will write your name, your age and "Nature Journal" - that's the Title of your book! Make sure your writing is neat and clean so that others can read it.

Step 2: Pages 1 and 2 come after the Title Page. This is called a "spread" because there are two pages "spread" together. Glue, tape or draw your Phenology wheel with 32 pie pieces onto one page of the spread. You will use this page each day to track the phases of the moon! Write in the dates of the month above the pie pieces. Please keep this page tidy (no doodling) so that your observations can be clearly notated. Now, paste your Phenology wheel on one of these pages. You pick which one! (On the other page you can use *Nature Study Hacking - Trees* guide to learn how to track trees throughout the year!)

Step 3: Flip to the back of your book. Starting with the last spread and working backwards (toward the front of your book), write the months of the year. I like to start with December, November etc and working my way into the center of the book until I come to January. This creates a "Perpetual Journal" where you can make entries about what you encounter during that month. You will be able to add a little bit to these pages over time. These entries can be about anything you find in nature and want to record into your Nature Journal (even if you aren't studying that topic!)

NatureStudyHacking.com

SIMPLE
LESSONS
START HERE

Moon's Phases Phenology Wheel| Lesson 1

Supply list:
1. A New Moon (preferred)
2. Nature Journal
3. Pencil and eraser
4. Preprinted Moon Phenology wheel (See the following page) sliced into 30 pie pieces for each month of the year (this is to track the moon this month)
5. Scissors
6. Tape or glue (to secure the Moon Phenology Wheel into your Nature Notebook) (unless you choose to draw one using a protractor, then you'll need a protractor!)

Step 1: In the front of your Natural Journal on the first two page spread paste/glue the Moon Phenology wheel to track the moon. The moon takes an average of 29.53 days to go through all of its phases. You will track the moon **everyday** (or as close to everyday as possible) for one month!

Step 2: On your Moon Phenology Wheel, draw the shape of the moon as it is today. Can you see it in the sky? If it's too cloudy to see, you'll need to use another source to make your recording for today. What can you use to find out what phase the moon is in today? Record the phase the moon is in and what the weather was like i.e. cloudy, rainy, snowy, sunny, partly cloudy etc. You may draw a picture if you'd prefer.

Note: Go to this website for phases of the moon: https://www.calendar-12.com/moon_calendar/

Moon Phases Phenology Wheel

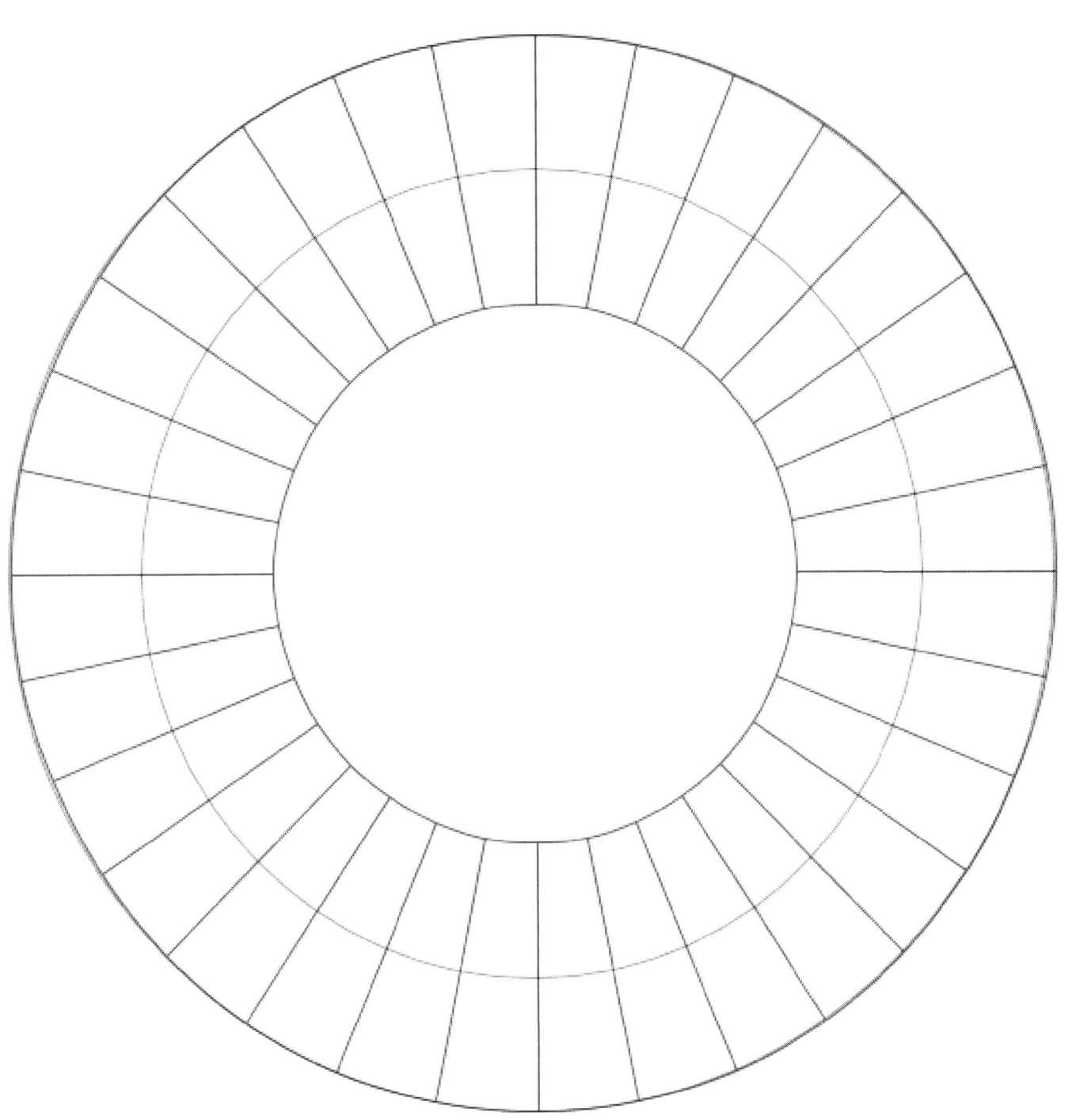

Moon's Phases Vocabulary| Lesson 2

Supply List:
1. Nature Journal
2. Pencil and eraser

Step 1: Today we will explore why the moon appears to change its shape from night to night.

Step 2: Read the following definitions out loud. Copy the words and definitions into your Nature Journal so that you can refer to them later.

Definitions:
Phases - the separate stages the moon according to how much light it reflects as seen from earth
Waxing - growing or swelling
Waning - shrinking or getting smaller
New Moon - when the unlit side of the moon is facing the earth
First Quarter - or half moon - when the moon is one quarter of the way through its orbit around the earth
Full Moon - the moon is halfway through its orbit around the earth. The lit side of the moon is facing the earth.
Third Quarter - The last quarter of the moon's cycle

Step 3: On your Moon Phenology Wheel, draw the shape of the moon as it is today. Record today's date along with the phase the moon is in and what the weather was like i.e. cloudy, rainy, snowy, sunny, partly cloudy etc. You may draw a picture if you'd prefer.

> **Younger students:** For very young students, Parents/Teachers should just pick one word for the child to copy. The rest will be picked up as you go through the month learning about the moon and anticipating the next phase.
>
> **Note:** This lesson may take two days to complete. Keep the lesson to less than 20 minutes.

Moon's Phases Demonstration | Lesson 3

Supply List:
1. Lamp or flashlight
2. 1 large apple or fruit
3. 1 small apple or fruit
4. Stick, pencil or rod (to attach the large apple to the small apple)
5. Stick, pencil or rod (to rotate the large apple)

Step 1: Now that you've been tracking the moon for at least one week, let's do an experiment to help us understand why the moon appears to change shape.

Does the moon have its own light? How do the earth and moon move together in space? How many days does it take the moon to orbit around the earth? How does the position of the moon affect what light we see reflected from earth? Why do we always see the same side of the moon?

Step 2: Attach the small apple to the large apple with the stick or rod. Then, insert the wire into the bottom of the large apple. Make the room dim so that you will be able to see the light from your lamp clearly shining on your apples posing as the earth and moon. (See next page for diagram.)

Step 3: Hold your apples up next to the light. Can you make an eclipse of the moon? (Let the shadow of the earth fall upon the moon.) Can you make an eclipse of the sun? (Move the moon apple between the sun and earth.)

Step 4: On your Moon Phenology Wheel, draw the shape of the moon as it is today. Record today's date along with the phase the moon is in and what the weather was like i.e. cloudy, rainy, snowy, sunny, partly cloudy etc. You may draw a picture if you'd prefer.

    Younger Students: Drawing is preferred at this age.

    Older Students: Writing and drawing can be used together.

Note: Go to this playlist to find a video explaining the phases of the moon: **https://tinyurl.com/y22vsp9x**

Moon Phases Demonstration

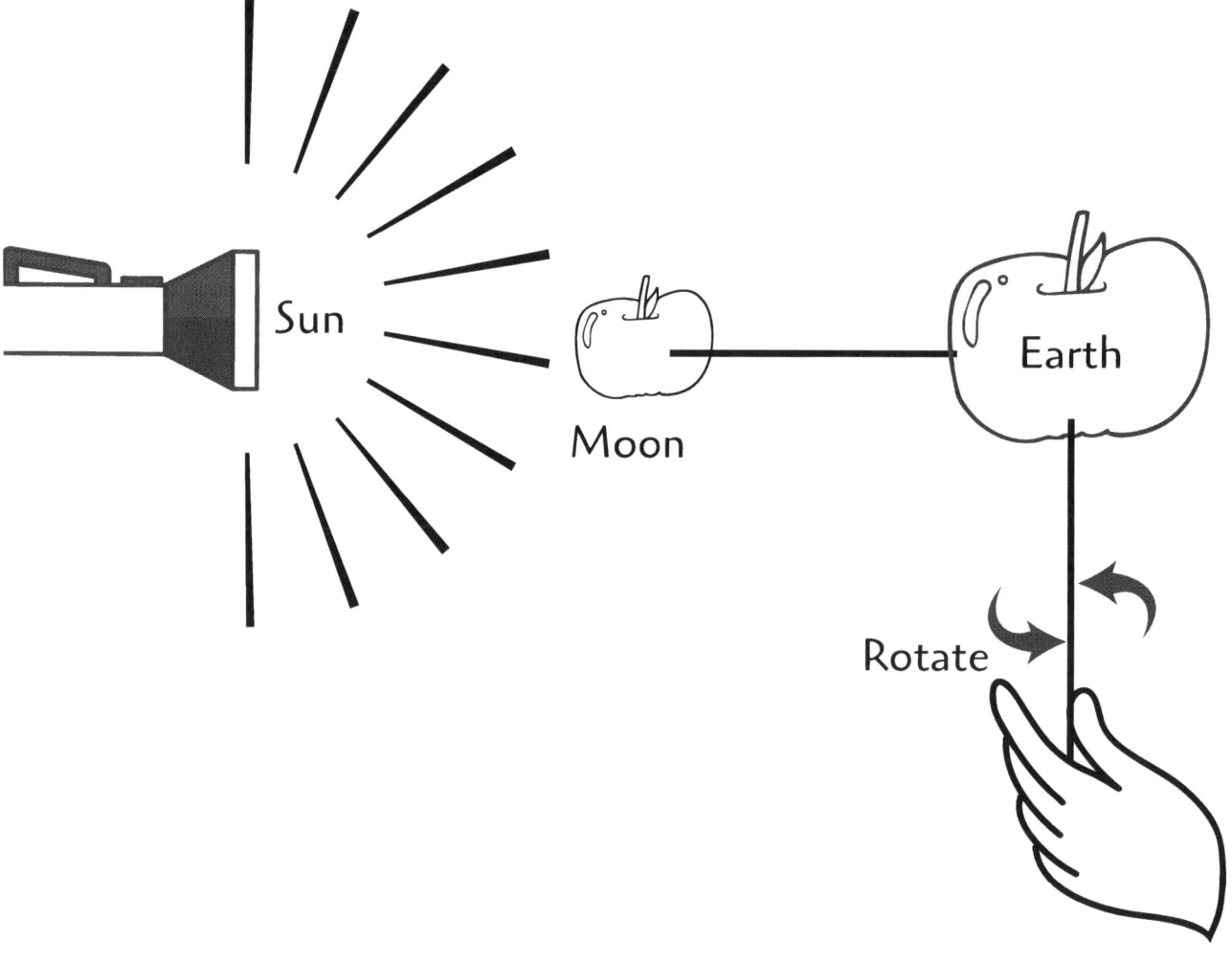

Moon Poem | Lesson 4

Supply List:
1. Nature Journal
2. *Nature Study Hacking - Stars & Skies* booklet

Step 1:. Select a poem about the moon that you like. On the next blank page of your Nature Journal, copy a verse or two from the poem. Write today's date and the name of the poem and page number you found the poem.

Step 2: On your Moon Phenology Wheel, draw the shape of the moon as it is today. Record today's date along with the phase the moon is in and what the weather was like i.e. cloudy, rainy, snowy, sunny, partly cloudy etc. You may draw a picture if you'd prefer.

Moon Poem Continued | Lesson 5

Supply List:
1. Nature Notebook
2. Pencil and eraser
3. Colored pencils or paints

Step 1: On the same page you copied your poem about the moon, draw a picture about the poem. (Don't forget to include the moon:)

Step 2: On your Moon Phenology Wheel, draw the shape of the moon as it is today. Record today's date along with the phase the moon is in and what the weather was like i.e. cloudy, rainy, snowy, sunny, partly cloudy etc. You may draw a picture if you'd prefer.

Moon - Reading | Lesson 6

Supply List:
1. A book about the moon (See Resources page for recommendations)
2. Nature Notebook
3. Pencils and eraser

Step 1: Read about the moon for five minutes or so. Copy something interesting or new you learned about the moon into your Nature Notebook.

Step 2: On your Moon Phenology Wheel, draw the shape of the moon as it is today. Record today's date along with the phase the moon is in and what the weather was like i.e. cloudy, rainy, snowy, sunny, partly cloudy etc. You may draw a picture if you'd prefer.

Review, Improve & Delight | Lesson 7

Supply List:
1. Nature Journal
2. Pencil and eraser
3. Pen (optional)
4. *Nature Study Hacking - Stars & Skies* booklet

Step 1: Copy the moon phases diagram from the next page into your Nature Journal. Can you name all the types of phases the moon goes through? Can you do it in their order starting with the New Moon?

Step 2: On your Moon Phenology Wheel, draw the shape of the moon as it is today. Record today's date along with the phase the moon is in and what the weather was like i.e. cloudy, rainy, snowy, sunny, partly cloudy etc. You may draw a picture if you'd prefer.

Phases of the Moon

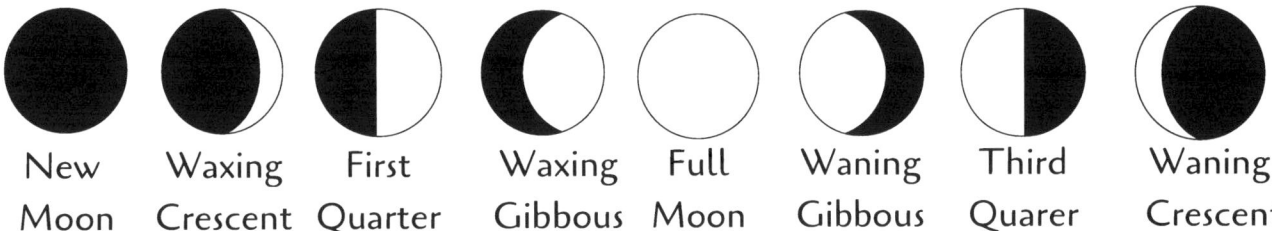

Moon Phenology Wheel| Lesson 8

Supply List:
1. Nature Journal
2. Pencil and eraser
3. Pen (optional)

Step 1: On your Moon Phenology Wheel, draw the shape of the moon as it is today. Record today's date along with the phase the moon is in and what the weather was like i.e. cloudy, rainy, snowy, sunny, partly cloudy etc. You may draw a picture if you'd prefer.

Step 2: If you've already drawn your phases of the moon in pencil, now you may outline the phases of the moon in pen. Fill in any days you may have missed in observing this month's phases of the moon.

Note: Go to this website for phases of the moon from the current month: https://www.farmersalmanac.com/calendar/moon-phases/

Big Dipper and Little Dipper - Story | Lesson 9

Supply List:
1. Pencil and eraser
2. Nature Notebook

Step 1: Read the story below about the Big Bear and Little Bear (commonly known as the Big Dipper and Little Dipper)

Step 2: In your Nature Notebook on the next blank page, draw a picture and write a sentence or two about the story.

Big Dipper and Little Dipper (Big Bear and Little Bear)

There is an ancient myth telling the story of the Big and Little Bears: A beautiful mother called Callisto had a little son whom she named Arcas. Callisto was so beautiful that she awakened the anger of Juno, who changed her to a bear; and when her son grew up he became a hunter, and one day would have killed his transformed mother; but Jupiter seeing the danger of this crime caught the two up into the heavens, and set them there as shining stars. But Juno was still vindictive, so she wrought a spell which never allowed these stars to rise and set like other stars, but kept them always moving around and around. (*Handbook of Nature Study*, p 823)

Younger Students: Parents/Teachers may write down oral retellings into a child's Nature Journal.

Older Students: Tell back the story of Big Bear and Little Bear in your own words. Who is Juno married to? Why was Juno angry?

Big Dipper and Little Dipper - Drawing | Lesson 10

Supply List:
1. Nature Notebook
2. Pencil and eraser

Step 1: In your Nature Notebook, on the same page you drew the a picture from the story about Big Bear and Little Bear draw a picture of the Big Dipper and Little Dipper. Please be sure to draw the same number of stars (or dots) as you see in the picture. See the next page for the diagram.

Step 2: This week when it is dark outside, go outside and see if you can locate the Big Dipper and Little Dipper. Can you find Polestar also known as the North Star?? *Hint: it's the star at the tip of the handle in the Little Dipper.*

Big Dipper and Little Dipper

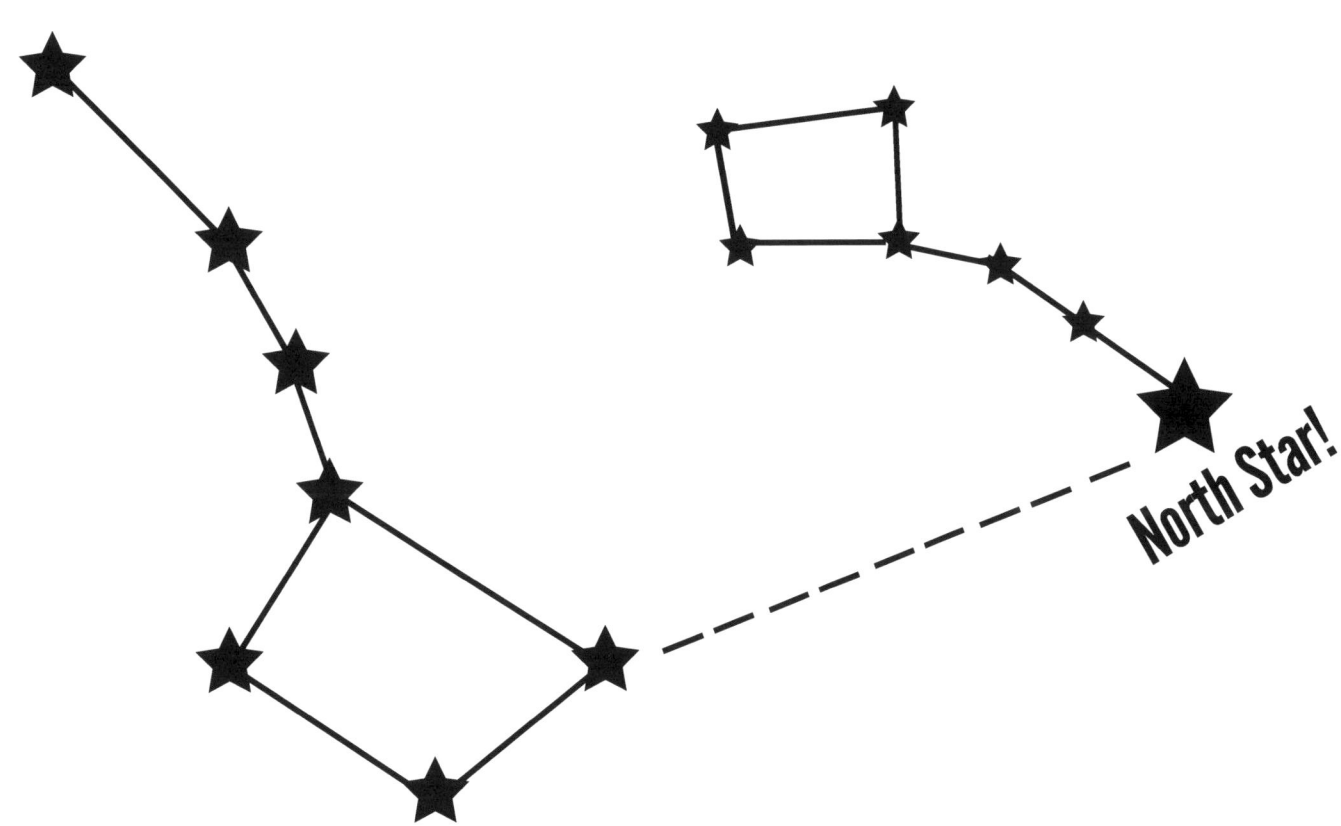

Review, Improve & Delight| Lesson 11

Supply List:
1. Nature Journal
2. Pencil and eraser
3. Colored Pencils or Watercolor Paints

Step 1: Open your Nature Journal. Look back at the work that you have done so far. Can you add to anything you've made? Can you make anything neater? Do you need to finish your poem or add to it? Erase extra pencil marks and trace pencil marks with ink that you like. This is your time to add color where you want and to improve the work that you've already done.

Cassiopeia's Chair - Story | Lesson 12

Supply List:
1. *Nature Study Hacking - Stars & Skies*
2. Pencil and eraser
3. Nature Notebook

Step 1: Read the story about Cassiopeia's Chair below.

Step 2: In your Nature Journal on the next blank page, draw a picture and write about the story.

Queen Cassiopeia's Chair is on the opposite side of the North Star from the Big Dipper and at about equal distance from it. It consists of five brilliant stars that form a W with the top toward Polaris, one-half of the being wider than the other. There is a less brilliant sixth star which finishes out half of the W into a chair seat, making of the figure a very uneasy looking throne for a poor queen to sit upon.

King Cepheus is Queen Cassiopeia's husband, and he sits with one foot on the North Star quite near to his royal spouse. His constellation is marked by five stars, four of which form a lozenge, and a line connecting the two stars on the side of the lozenge farthest from Cassiopeia, if extended, will reach the North Star as surely as a line from the Big Dipper pointers.

Cepheus is not such a shining light in the heavens as is his wife, for his stars are not so brilliant. Perhaps this is because he was only incidentally put in the skies. He was merely the consort of Queen Cassiopeia, who being a vain and jealous lady boasted that she and her daughter, Andromeda, were far more beautiful than any other goddesses that ever were, and thus incurred the wrath of Juno and Jupiter who set the whole family "sky high" and quite out of the way, a punishment which must have had its compensations since they are where the world of men may look at and admire them for all ages. (*Handbook of Nature Study*, p 894-895)

Cassiopeia's Chair - Drawing | Lesson 13

Supply List:
1. Nature Notebook
2. Pencil and eraser

Step 1: In your Nature Journal, on the same page you drew the a picture from the story about Cassiopeia's Chair, copy the picture of the constellation from the following page. Please be sure to draw the same number of stars (or dots) as you see in the picture. See the next page for the diagram.

Step 2: This week when it is dark outside, go outside and see if you can locate the Cassiopeia. Can you find it in relation to the Big Dipper?

Cassiopeia's Chair

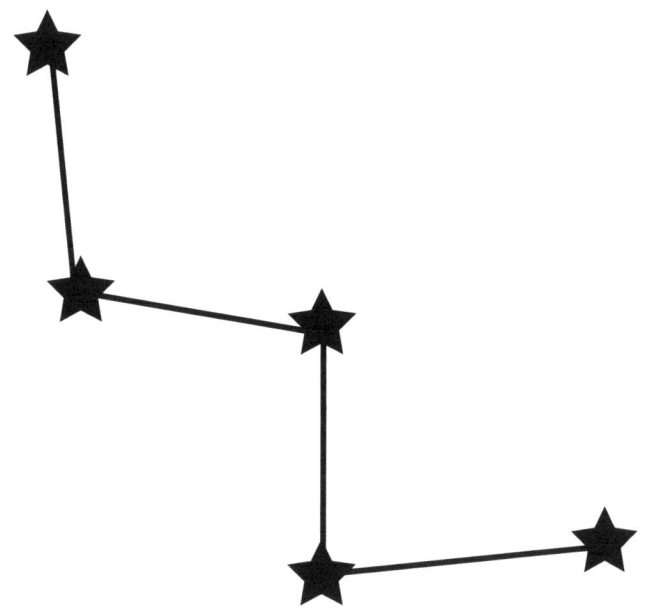

Perpetual Journal Entry| Lesson 14

Supply List:
1. Nature Journal
2. Pencil and eraser
3. Book of Poetry or *Nature Study Hacking* book

Step 1: Go outside for five minutes and pay attention to the weather, sights and sounds.

Step 2: In your Nature Journal, in the back you wrote the names of the months. Under the current month, draw or write about today's weather. What are the sounds you hear? What do you see up? What do you see down? Sit quietly and pay attention. What does the weather feel like? Do you like it? If it's too hot or cold to be outside for too long, step outside and feel how the temperature hits you.

Step 3: In the back of your Nature Journal, under section for this month, write down your observations from your time outside today.

Orion - Story | Lesson 15

Supply List:
1. Pencil and eraser
2. Nature Journal

Step 1: Read about the constellation Orion below.

Step 2: In your Nature Journal on the next blank page, draw a picture and write about what you read.

Orion is a constellation which almost everyone knows; three stars in a row outline his belt, and a curving line of stars, set obliquely below the belt, outlines the sword. In this constellation the ancients saw Orion, the great hunter, with his belt and his sword; Betelgeuse was set like a glowing ruby on his shoulder, and the white star Rigel was set like a spur on his heel. Thus stood the great hunter in the sky, with his club raised to keep off the plunging bull whose eye is the red Aldebaran (al-deb'a-ran).

The three beautiful stars which make; Orion's belt are all double stars; the belt Orion, the three large stars in a line forming the belt, the curved line of smaller stars below forming the sword, Betelgeuse above to the left, Rigel below the belt, forming with Betelgeuse and the three stars of the belt a long narrow diamond in the sky is just three degrees long and is a good unit for sky measurement. The sword is not merely the three stars which we ordinarily see, but is really a curved line of five stars; and what seems to be a hazy star, third from the tip of the sword is in fact a great nebula. Through the telescope this nebula seems a splash of light
with six beautiful stars within it. (*Handbook of Nature Study*, p. 823)

Orion - Drawing| Lesson 16

Supply List:
1. Nature Notebook
2. Pencil and eraser

Step 1: In your Nature Journal, on the same page you drew the a picture from the story about Orion copy the constellation of Orion. Please be sure to draw the same number of stars as you see in the picture. See the diagram on the next page.

Step 2: This week when it is dark outside, go outside and see if you can locate Orion. Can you find his belt?

Orion the Hunter

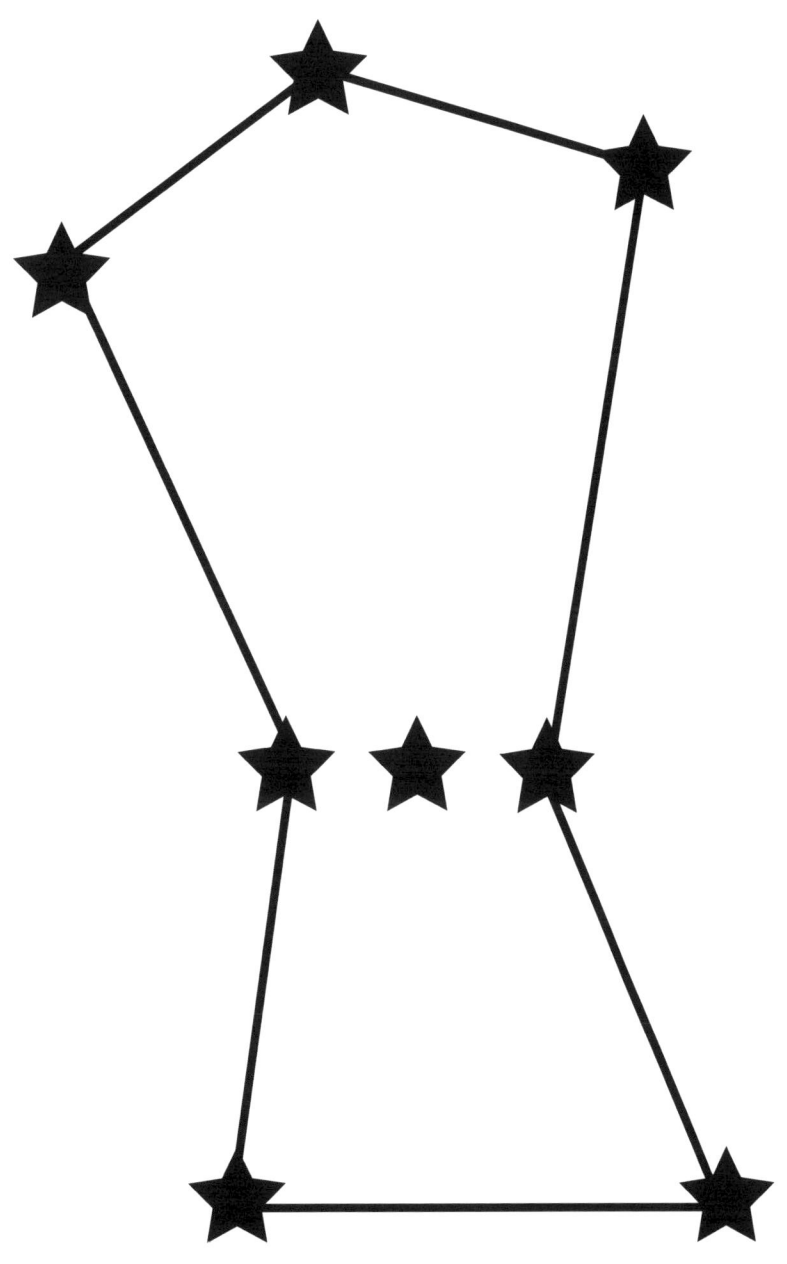

Stars Poem | Lesson 17

Supply List:
1. Nature Journal
2. *Nature Study Hacking - Stars & Skies* booklet

Step 1:. Select a poem about the stars that you like. On the next blank page of your Nature Journal, copy a verse or two from the poem. Write today's date and the name and author of the poem.

Step 2: Go back through your entries about the stars. Can you add to them? Make them neater? Erase extra lines? Go back over them with pen? This is the time to work on the quality of your work.

Planets - Drawing| Lesson 18

Supply List:
1. Nature Notebook
2. Pencil and eraser

Step 1: In your Nature Notebook on the next blank page draw each of the planets. Make sure you label them so you can remember which ones you've already drawn. See the following page for the diagram of the planets.

Step 2: This week when it is dark outside, go outside and see if you can locate some of the planets.

***Hint**: Planets Visible in January : with naked eye, Mercury, Venus, Mars, Jupiter and Saturn are visible. In a telescope, Uranus and Neptune are visible as tiny discs.*

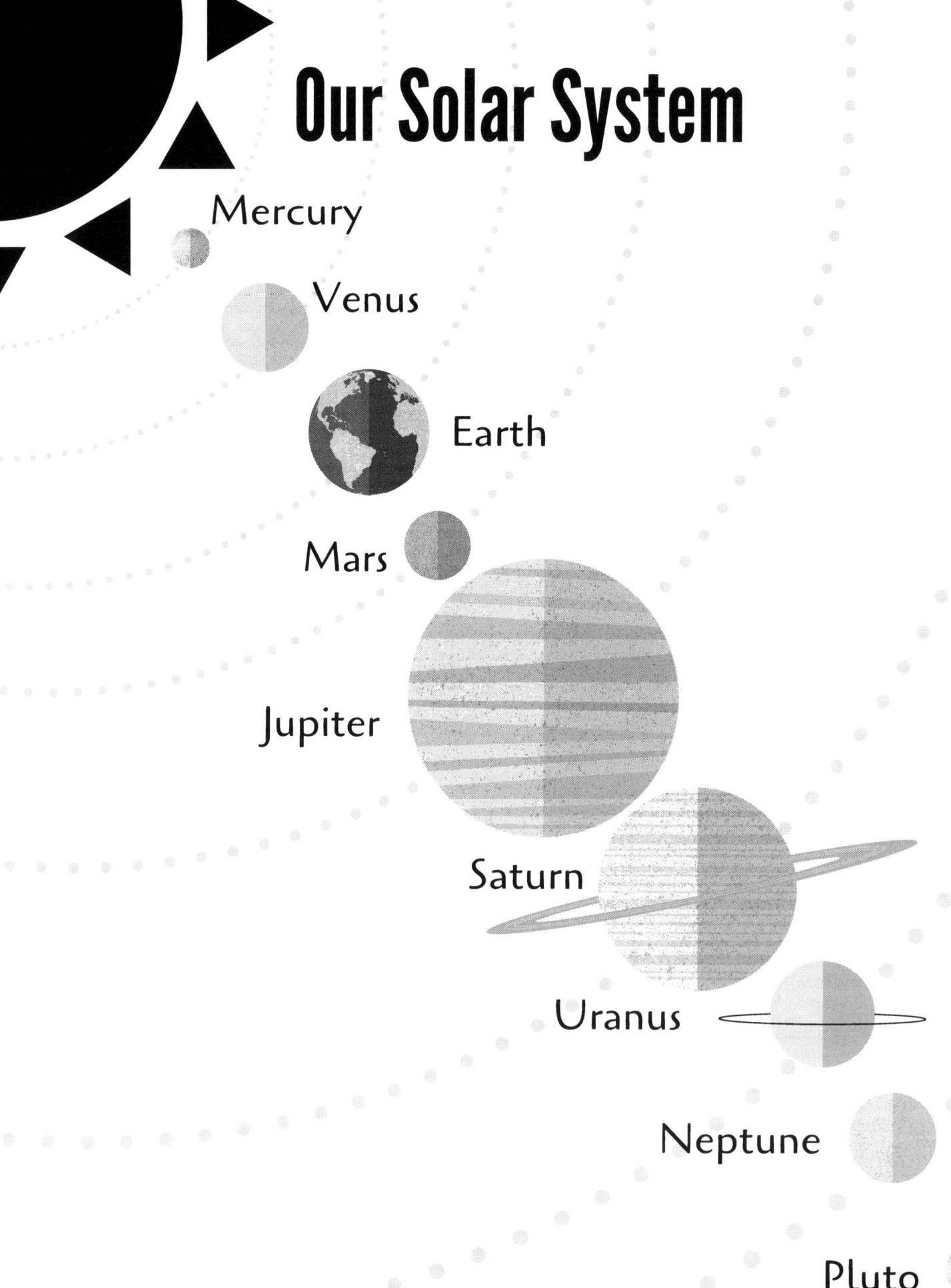

Review, Improve & Delight | Lesson 19

Supply List:
1. Nature Journal
2. Pencil and eraser

Step 1: Continue working on your Solar System. Add to the details and clean up your markings. Erase extra pencil marks.

Sun Makes a Shadow | Lesson 20

Supply List:
1. Nature Journal
2. Pencil and eraser

Step 1: Go outside in the MORNING and look at the shadows on the ground. Find one plant or object that has a shadow to draw into your Nature Journal. Draw a sketch of the object and its shadow.

Step 2: Write down the time and date you made your drawing.

Sun Makes a Shadow Continued| Lesson 21

Supply List:
1. Nature Notebook
2. Pencil and eraser
3. Colored pencils (optional)

Step 1: Go outside in the AFTERNOON and look at the shadows on the ground. Draw the plant or object you drew on Day 1 into Nature Notebook. Draw a sketch of the object and its shadow. Pay attention to where the shadow is now. Has it changed? In what direction did it change?

Step 2: Write down the time and date you made your drawing.

Sun Makes the Seasons| Lesson 22

Supply List:
1. Nature Notebook
2. Pencil and eraser

Step 1: In your Nature Notebook on the next blank page copy the diagram that shows how the sun makes the seasons on the earth. Make sure you label them so you can remember which ones you've already drawn. See the next page for the diagram.

Step 2: Label which hemisphere is winter and which is summer depending on how the sun's rays are hitting the earth.

> **Note:** Go to this playlist to find a video about how the sun makes the seasons:
> https://tinyurl.com/y22vsp9x

How the Sun makes the Seasons

Earth is tilted in the same direction as it orbits the sun.
The sun's light shines differently on the earth at different times of the year.
Winter is cooler because the sun's rays are hitting that part of the earth less directly.
Summer is warmer because the earth is tilted toward the sun.
The sun's rays are hitting that part of the earth more directly.

Winter in the Northern Hemosphere Summer in the Northern Hemosphere
Summer in the Southern Hemosphere Winter in the Southern Hemosphere

Perpetual Journal Entry| Lesson 23

Supply List:
1. Nature Journal
2. Pencil and eraser
3. Book of Poetry or *Nature Study Hacking* book

Step 1: Go outside for five minutes and pay attention to the weather, sights and sounds.

Step 2: In your Nature Journal, in the back you wrote the names of the months. Under the current month, draw or write about today's weather. What are the sounds you hear? What do you see up? What do you see down? Sit quietly and pay attention. What does the weather feel like? Do you like it? If it's too hot or cold to be outside for too long, step outside and feel how the temperature hits you.

Step 3: In the back of your Nature Journal, under section for this month, write down your observations from your time outside today.

Review, Improve & Delight | Lesson 24

Supply List:
1. Nature Journal
2. Pencil and eraser
3. Colored Pencils or Watercolor Paints

Step 1: Open your Nature Journal. Look back at the work that you have done so far. Can you add to anything you've made? Can you make anything neater? Do you need to finish your poem or add to it? Erase extra pencil marks and trace pencil marks with ink that you like. This is your time to add color where you want and to improve the work that you've already done.

STARS & SKIES | Exam Week

Supply List:
1. Nature Journal
2. Pencils and eraser

Step 1: Look through your Nature Journal you created this year. Look at the pages where you recorded the phases of the moon, the constellations you discovered and the sun's relationship to the earth. Spend about 5-10 minutes.

Step 2: Tell your parent about the moon, stars or sun. You may use your Nature Journal to demonstrate and show examples of what you remember. Be sure to include the most interesting thing that you learned.

(Note to parent: you may choose to write down what your child says or record their narration on video.)

Poems about Stars & Skies

De Profundis
by Christina Rossetti

Oh why is heaven built so far,
Oh why is earth set so remote?
I cannot reach the nearest star
That hangs afloat.

I would not care to reach the moon,
One round monotonous of change;
Yet even she repeats her tune
Beyond my range.

I never watch the scatter'd fire
Of stars, or sun's far-trailing train,
But all my heart is one desire,
And all in vain:

For I am bound with fleshly bands,
Joy, beauty, lie beyond my scope;
I strain my heart, I stretch my hands,
And catch at hope.

**The Moon's the North Wind's Cooky
(What the little girl said)**
Vachel Lindsay

The Moon's the North Wind's cooky.
He bites it, day by day,
Until there's but a rim of scraps,
That crumble all away.

The South Wind is a baker.
He kneads clouds in his den,
And bakes a crisp new moon that...greedy
North...Wind...eats...again!

Windy Nights
by Robert Louis Stevenson

Whenever the moon and stars are set,
Whenever the wind is high,
All night long in the dark and wet,
A man goes riding by.
Late in the night when the fires are out,
Why does he gallop and gallop about?

Whenever the trees are crying aloud,
And ships are tossed at sea,
By, on the highway, low and loud,
By at the gallop goes he.
By at the gallop he goes, and then
By he comes back at the gallop again.

My Shadow

by Robert Louis Stevenson

I have a little shadow that goes in and out with me,
And what can be the use of him is more than I can see.
He is very, very like me from the heels up to the head;
And I see him jump before me, when I jump into my bed.

The funniest thing about him is the way he likes to grow—
Not at all like proper children, which is always very slow;
For he sometimes shoots up taller like an india-rubber ball,
And he sometimes gets so little that there's none of him at all.

He hasn't got a notion of how children ought to play,
And can only make a fool of me in every sort of way.
He stays so close beside me, he's a coward you can see;
I'd think shame to stick to nursie as that shadow sticks to me!

One morning, very early, before the sun was up,
I rose and found the shining dew on every buttercup;
But my lazy little shadow, like an arrant sleepy-head,
Had stayed at home behind me and was fast asleep in bed.

The Star

by Jane Taylor

Twinkle, twinkle, little star,
How I wonder what you are!
Up above the world so high,
Like a diamond in the sky.

When the blazing sun is gone,
When he nothing shines upon,
Then you show your little light,
Twinkle, twinkle, all the night.

Then the traveller in the dark,
Thanks you for your tiny spark,
He could not see which way to go,
If you did not twinkle so.

In the dark blue sky you keep,
And often through my curtains peep,
For you never shut your eye,
Till the sun is in the sky.

'Tis your bright and tiny spark,
Lights the traveller in the dark :
Though I know not what you are,
Twinkle, twinkle, little star.

A Winter Night
by Sara Teasdale

My window-pane is starred with frost,
The world is bitter cold to-night,
The moon is cruel and the wind
Is like a two-edged sword to smite.

God pity all the homeless ones,
The beggars pacing to and fro.
God pity all the poor to-night
Who walk the lamp-lit streets of snow.

The Faery Forest
by Sara Teasdale

The faery forest glimmered
    Beneath an ivory moon,
The silver grasses shimmered
    Against a faery tune.

Beneath the silken silence
    The crystal branches slept,
And dreaming through the dew-fall
    The cold white blossoms wept.

Good Night! Good Night!
By Victor Hugo

Good night! Good night!
Far flies the light;
But still God's love
Shall flame above,
Making all bright.
Good night! Good night!

The Kind Moon
by Sara Teasdale

I think the moon is very kind
    To take such trouble just for me.
He came along with me from home
    To keep me company.
He went as fast as I could run;
    I wonder how he crossed the sky?
I'm sure he hasn't legs and feet
    Or any wings to fly.
Yet here he is above their roof;
    Perhaps he thinks it isn't right
For me to go so far alone,
    Though mother said I might.

Evening
by Emily Dickinson

The cricket sang,
And set the sun,
And workmen finished, one by one,
    Their seam the day upon.

The low grass loaded with the dew,
The twilight stood as strangers do
With hat in hand, polite and new,
    To stay as if, or go.

A vastness, as a neighbor, came,
A wisdom without face or name,
A peace, as hemispheres at home,
    And so the night became.

Lady Moon
 by Richard Monckton Milnes

"Lady Moon, Lady Moon, where are you roving?"
    "Over the sea."
"Lady Moon, Lady Moon, whom are you loving?"
    "All that love me."

"Are you not tired with rolling and never
    Resting to sleep?
Why look so pale and so sad, as for ever
    Wishing to weep?"

"Ask me not this, little child, if you love me;
    You are too bold.
I must obey my dear Father above me,
    And do as I'm told."

"Lady Moon, Lady Moon, where are you roving?"
    "Over the sea."
"Lady Moon, Lady Moon, whom are you loving?"
    "All that love me."

The Wind and the Moon
by George Macdonald

Said the Wind to the Moon, "I will blow you out.
    You stare
      In the air
        Like a ghost in a chair,
Always looking what I am about;
I hate to be watched--I'll blow you out."

The Wind blew hard, and out went the Moon.
    So deep,
      On a heap
        Of clouds, to sleep,
Down lay the Wind, and slumbered soon--
Muttering low, "I've done for that Moon."

He turned in his bed; she was there again!
    On high
      In the sky
        With her one ghost eye,
The Moon shone white and alive and plain.
Said the Wind--"I will blow you out again."

The Wind blew hard, and the Moon grew dim.
    "With my sledge
      And my wedge
        I have knocked off her edge!
If only I blow right fierce and grim,
The creature will soon be dimmer than dim."

He blew and he blew, and she thinned to a thread.
    "One puff
      More's enough
        To blow her to snuff!
One good puff more where the last was bred,
And glimmer, glimmer, glum will go the thread!"

He blew a great blast, and the thread was gone;
    In the air
      Nowhere
        Was a moonbeam bare;
Far off and harmless the shy stars shone;
Sure and certain the Moon was gone.

The Wind, he took to his revels once more;
    On down
      In town,
        Like a merry-mad clown,
He leaped and hallooed with whistle and roar,
"What's that?" The glimmering thread once more!

He flew in a rage--he danced and blew;
    But in vain
      Was the pain
        Of his bursting brain;
For still the broader the Moon-scrap grew,
The broader he swelled his big cheeks and blew.

Slowly she grew--till she filled the night,
    And shone
      On her throne
        In the sky alone,
A matchless, wonderful, silvery light,
Radiant and lovely, the Queen of the night.

Said the Wind--"What a marvel of power am I!
    With my breath,
      Good faith!
        I blew her to death--
First blew her away right out of the sky--
Then blew her in; what strength have I!"

But the Moon, she knew nothing about the affair,
    For high
      In the sky,
        With her one white eye,
Motionless, miles above the air,
She had never heard the great Wind blare.

The Sunshine

by Mary Howitt

I love the sunshine everywhere--
    In wood and field, and glen;
I love it in the busy haunts
    Of town-imprisoned men.

I love it when it streameth in
    The humble cottage door,
And casts the chequered casement-shade
    Upon the red brick floor.

I love it where the children lie
    Deep in the clovery grass,
To watch among the twining roots
    The gold-green beetle pass.

How beautiful, where dragon-flies
    Are wondrous to behold,
With rainbow wings of gauzy pearl,
    And bodies blue and gold!

How beautiful on harvest-slopes
    To see the sunshine lie;
Or on the paler reaped fields
    Where yellow shocks stand high!

I love it, on the breezy sea,
    To glance on sail and oar,
While the great waves, like molten glass,
    Come leaping to the shore.

Oh! yes; I love the sunshine!
    Like kindness or like mirth,
Upon a human countenance
    Is sunshine on the earth!

Upon the earth; upon the sea;
    And through the crystal air,
On piled up clouds; the gracious sun;
    Is glorious everywhere.

What do the stars do

by Christina Rossetti

What do the stars do
    Up in the sky,
Higher than the wind can blow,
    Or the clouds can fly?

Each star in its own glory
    Circles, circles still;
As it was lit to shine and set,
    And do its Maker's will.

Resources

For clickable links visit
www.naturestudyhacking.com/stars-skies-resources-and-links/

Nature Study Essentials:
Handbook of Nature Study by Anna Comstock
Nature Anatomy by Julia Rothman

Introduction to Stars, Moon, Seasons and Planets:
A Walk through the Heavens: A Guide to Stars and Constellations and their Legends by Milton D. Heifetz
The Planets by Gail Gibbons
The Reason for Seasons by Gail Gibbons
The Moon Book by Gail Gibbons

Reference books about Stars & Skies:
Audubon Society Field Guide to the Night Sky

Nature Drawing help for early elementary:
How to Draw Almost Everything by Chika Miyata

PNEU Articles on Nature Study as inspiration:

https://www.amblesideonline.org/PR/PR07p332NaturalHistory.shtml
https://www.amblesideonline.org/PR/PR41p000CharmNatureStudy.shtml

Handbook of Nature Study:
The Skies, p. 815-859

YouTube Playlist:
https://tinyurl.com/y22vsp9x

Supply List:
1. Minimalism Art Dot grid notebook (8.5/11 size preferred for younger children)
2. Ticonderoga pencils
3. Prisma colored pencils (preferred for younger children)
4. Preprinted Phenology wheel sliced into 32 pie pieces for each day month (plus one space for the month's name)
5. Scissors
6. Tape or glue

(Continued on next page)

7. Protractor (optional if making phenology wheel instead of printing/copying it from book)
8. The night sky, sun and moon
9. Book about the Moon, Stars, Planets and Seasons (See Resources page for recommended readings)
10. Night Sky App (point at the sky and it tells you what star/planet/constellation you are observing!)

About the Author

Joy Cherrick is wife to her entrepreneurial husband, Kevin, and is mother and home educator to their six children. She classically homeschools her children using the Charlotte Mason method. Joy loves learning new things, being a supportive friend and being outside. She can usually be found at home, her favorite place to work and rest. You can find her online at litandlilies.com.

Books in the
Nature Study Hacking Series

Nature Study Hacking - Trees

Nature Study Hacking - Stars & Skies

Nature Study Hacking - Weather, Wind and Water

Nature Study Hacking - Cultivated Crops & Weeds

Get updates about when we release new books by signing up at

NatureStudyHacking.com

#naturestudyhacking

Terms of Use:
Copyright Joy Cherrick All right reserved.
You may not create anything to sell or share based on this product.
This product is for one teacher use only.
All poems used herein are in the public domain.
Designed and formatted by Joy Cherrick.

(The downloadable version of this document contains affiliate links)

Made in the USA
Columbia, SC
08 January 2021